*Gift, Mystery, and Calling*

ᔆ   ᔆ   ᔆ

# Gift, Mystery, and Calling

## *Prayers and Reflections*

by Robert Morneau

Featuring the poetry of Brother Edward Seifert, FSC
with photography by Anne Egan

Saint Mary's Press
Christian Brothers Publications
Winona, Minnesota

The publishing team included Carl Koch, development editor; Rebecca Fairbank, copy editor; Barbara Bartelson, production editor and typesetter; Stephan Nagel, cover designer; Anne Egan, photographer; pre-press, printing, and binding by the graphics division of Saint Mary's Press.

Cover painting: *The Starry Night* (1889), by Vincent van GOGH, oil on canvas, 29 by 36-¼ inches. The Museum of Modern Art, New York. Acquired through the Lillie P. Bliss Bequest. Photograph © 1994 by the Museum of Modern Art, New York.

The psalms in this book are from *Psalms Anew: In Inclusive Language,* compiled by Nancy Schreck and Maureen Leach (Winona, MN: Saint Mary's Press, 1986). Copyright © 1986 by Saint Mary's Press. All rights reserved.

The scriptural material found on pages 14 and 52 is freely adapted to make it inclusive regarding gender. These adaptations are not to be understood or used as official translations of the Bible.

All other scriptural quotations in this book are from the New Jerusalem Bible. Copyright © 1985 by Darton, Longman and Todd, London; and Doubleday, a division of Bantam, Doubleday, Dell Publishing Group, New York. Used with permission.

Acknowledgments continue on page 109.

Printed in the United States of America

Printing: 9 8 7 6 5 4 3 2

Year: 2002 01 00 99 98 97 96

ISBN 0-88489-346-4 paper
0-88489-355-3 spiral-bound

 Genuine recycled paper with 10% post-consumer waste.
Printed with soy-based ink.

# Contents

# Preface

The prayers and reflections in this book revolve around the poem-prayers of Br. Edward Seifert, a De La Salle Christian Brother. Some of his poems were published in books of his collected verse or in magazines like *America, Emmanuel,* and *Commonweal.* However, only a few of Edward's friends have read most of his poems. This book of prayers and reflections offers you a chance to pray along with this quiet, unassuming, insightful, and sensitive brother. I hope that such an adventure will enrich your life as much as it has my own.

I had the privilege of knowing Edward for twenty years. He would often send me a fresh poem, asking for comments and suggestions as to where he might submit it for publication. He had a poetic gift that came to full flower later in his life. His young adulthood and middle age were spent in the active, demanding ministry of teaching, leaving him too little energy for writing.

Born in 1911, Brother Edward grew up in Milwaukee, took his bachelor's and master's degrees at Marquette University, and, at age twenty-nine, entered the novitiate of the De La Salle Christian Brothers. For the next twenty years, Edward taught English and religion in the brothers' schools in the Midwest. Finally, in 1959, when he became a school librarian, Edward began to write consistently, both prose and verse.

Edward wrote poetry up until the time of his death in 1990. Most of the poems reflect on the everyday life of a man, a brother, and a teacher as he gropes with the big questions of life in his own humble way. Some of the poems bite, others weep, some dance, and others ponder. They appeal to us because they reflect the range of reactions most of us have to the mysteries of living.

Edward bemoaned the seeming demise of religious poetry. In 1988 he wrote to me: "What is the situation of religious poetry? Not good, as far as I can see. The literary editor of *America* selects poems with an entirely secular theme. He seems to fear that a religious theme will necessarily be pietistic. Apparently he has not become too familiar with great religious poets such as Jessica Powers, Hopkins, Eliot, and others." The poems of Edward Seifert are far from pietistic. Like the Psalms, they speak plainly and from the heart.

Poetry was a kind of mystery to Edward. At his golden jubilee as a brother, he remarked: "My poetry is for me experience. I go to my files and try to lift them, they are so heavy. For me they represent what is good in my life, especially my friendships. My friends have been the mainstays of my life." I hope that when you pray with Edward, he can be a spiritual friend to you, as he is to me.

## How to Use the Prayers

Whether you use the prayers alone or with a group, try to create a prayerful mood with candles, an open Bible, or a crucifix. If a quiet place is not available, know that a loving God is present everywhere.

Begin by silently recalling God's presence. If you feel restless or rushed, spend some moments simply relaxing your body—letting go of all the tensions of the day, all the time demands, all your projects. Breathe deeply and slowly. A period of meditative breathing in God's presence is a prayer of simple attention. If you find it helpful, repeat a short prayer phrase in harmony with your breathing. For example, "You are present, Holy Friend." When you are present to God, engage in the rest of the prayer.

Pray each of the sections carefully, letting the meaning of the words take form for you. Each word and phrase is an offering to God. Give your offering deliberately. Pause in silence between each section. Go slowly—very slowly.

The prayers may be freely adapted to meet your needs. For instance, you may want to add a song at the start or end of a prayer. Other suggestions follow.

The opening prayer, hymn, readings, canticle, and closing prayer may be used in a variety of ways by a community. For instance, you may wish to have one person read the opening and closing prayers. The hymn may be recited in unison or by each member of the group reciting one or two lines. After the pause or reading, you may want to share reflections or petitions. The canticle may be done by having all pray the response and one person recite the verses. Vary the way in which the prayers are offered, but be sure to include everyone.

## Using the Food for Meditation, Journaling, or Sharing

Give *lectio divina* a try. *Lectio divina* means "divine studying," a concentrated reflection on the wisdom of a piece of writing. Read a selection from the section called "Food for Meditation, Journaling, or Sharing" (the reflection or either one of the poems). Then concentrate on one or two sentences or phrases, pondering their meaning for you. Next, read the piece again, slowly and meditatively. Follow this reading with a prayer or a conversation with God in reaction to the reading. Finally, read the selection once more and then compose your thoughts about it. *Lectio divina* commonly ends with the formulation of a resolution.

Undertake some journaling. Writing is a process of discovery. If you write for any length of time, stating honestly what is on your mind and in your heart, you will unearth much about who you are, how you stand with your God, what deep longings reside in your soul, and more. If you have never used writing as a means of prayer, try it. After you have spent time with a selection, write your response in some form, like a letter back to the author, a poem, a song, or a dialog with God. Questions are provided at the end of each poem. These might be good starting points for journaling.

**Reflect with a group**. If you are using the prayers in a group, you might begin the session with the prayer service. Then use the reflection or one or both of the poems for faith sharing. The questions may inspire discussion.

# A Final Word

I express gratitude to four individuals who assisted in the production of this book: Sr. Mary de Sales Hoffman, OSF, and Sr. Marie Isabel McElrone, OSF, for their kind but candid critiques; Anne Egan, whose photographs have enriched this volume; and Carl Koch, FSC, for spending extensive time editing these pages.

Of course, there is a fifth person: Br. Edward Seifert, FSC, poet, friend, and inspiration. My hope is that his creative work may enrich the hearts of many.

Bishop Robert Morneau
Green Bay, Wisconsin

❧  ❧  ❧

# *Gift*

## ∾ *1* ∾

# *The Gift of Life*

**Opening Prayer**

Gracious God, please give us the grace to see life in its totality. Just as we meet you on the mountains, may we find and serve you joyfully in the valleys.

# Hymn

What is it like to live on the ridge
and take in one sweep of seeing
the russet, the brown, and the orange
riding the curves of the hills,
to see the great river, the islands
afloat through dense leaves on the river,
and beyond them the bluffs, the lean
and the thrust of them, and the cloud banks?

You say you would like it, life
on the ridge, but not I.
It would be like listening to Bach
cantatas all the day long,
transcendent music from breakfast to teatime.
It would be like playing
contemplative hour after hour,
standing on tiptoe there on the ridge edge.

It is better to ride the road
downward into the valley,
to doze and then quietly remember
how the ridge lifted and held me
in a sudden look at creation.

("On the Ridge")

# God's Word

Jesus went out to the mountain to pray, spending the night in
communion with God. At daybreak he called his disciples and
selected twelve of them to be his Apostles. . . . Coming
down the mountain with them, he stopped at the level stretch
where there were many of his disciples; a large crowd of
people with them from all Judea and Jerusalem and the coast
of Tyre and Sidon, people who came to hear him and be
healed of their diseases. (Adapted from Luke 6:12–18)

**Pause**: Silently praise God for the Word and for God's
healing presence on the peaks and in the valleys.

# Reading

[A teacher] taught me one thing, . . . that life must be used in the service of a cause greater than oneself. This can be done by a Christian for two reasons: one is obedience to [God], the other is purely pragmatic, namely that one is going to miss the meaning of life if one doesn't. . . .

   And I must have caught it thoroughly, because in the course of a life which I have not considered conspicuously good, I have never given up on *trying to be obedient,* nor have I ever lost the pragmatic belief that I was going to miss something of the greatest importance if I did not treat my life as not being altogether my own property. (Alan Paton, *Towards the Mountain,* p. 59)

# Canticle

℟ Downward into the valley
   Downward into the valley

Farewell to the ridge and its transcendent music
Farewell to aloof living and its rarefied altitude
Farewell to beauty, distant-seen but unembraced

℟ Downward into the valley
   Downward into the valley

Welcome to colors, surrounding the breathless soul
Welcome to the river's rich giving waters
Welcome to islands where work must be done

℟ Downward into the valley
   Downward into the valley

Where tiptoe is changed into steps firm and strong
Where memory holds a meaningful vision
Where eye finds hope in bluffs and cloud banks

℟ Downward into the valley
   Downward into the valley

**Closing Prayer**

Gracious God, please give us the grace to see life in its totality.
God of heights and God of valleys,
you exalt our spirits with glorious transcendence,
(ah, the mystery of a spring day or autumn's full moon)
and you humble our hearts with the scandal of particularity
(how can an amoeba praise you?).
In you there is no abstraction,
your grace comes only in finite doses.
Renew our call to service,
give us Gethsemane courage to find you
in your valley designs and desires.
May your Calvary deed lift us over the threshold of fear
and place us firmly in the garden of love.
In Jesus' name we pray.
Amen. Alleluia!

# *Food for Meditation, Journaling, or Sharing*

## *Reflection*

During a spring break, philosophy books abandoned in favor of spring's call, I traveled with friends along the Blue Ridge Mountains of Virginia. The beauty was breathtaking: immense vistas, tiny bluebells, ancient oaks whispering their histories, the rich blue of the sky, gentle breezes filled with April joy and hope. Five days of travel and conversation, leisure and no responsibilities.

A fantasy crossed my mind: build a small cottage on a solitary bluff, learn organic gardening, gather my favorite music and books, and live a life free from the frantic pressures of our hurried and violent times. Fantasy indeed, sheer escapism and avoidance of responsibility. But what a way to go—Bach all day long and peaceful contemplation.

Eventually our car made its way back to the university. Schedules resumed, term papers came due, exams loomed around each corner, chores chewed up time, friends and acquaintances asked for help—the idyllic ridge was now a distant memory and the valley re-experienced. In our philosophical ponderings, my friends and I would often debate the questions: What is reality? Is it the vision from the ridge or the muddiness of the valley? Or is there a third world we are seeing? If not, how can we straddle the rarefied ideal and the devouring quotidian events we call history?

If it is better to ride the road downward into the valley, is it "good" to ascend the ridge to regain one's perspective and not forget about the what-can-be-ness of life? If the ridge is good and the valley is better, then what is best—a dose of Bach several times a week, a half hour of contemplation daily, encounters with the disheartened and lost on a regular basis? Our search for the best of all possible worlds may be too grand. Lowering our sights to the better, even the good, may perhaps suffice.

The ridge opens the door to transcendence, and the valley exposes us to the mystery of the Incarnation. Both geographies are necessary for a full life. Sacred are the heights, holy the lowlands. To limit our place to what is safe or desirable is to risk missing the joy of living.

Life on the ridge. Life down in the valley. Life in all the in-between places on our fragile planet earth.

## "Public Library Saturday Afternoon"

Hiding behind a double spread
of fancy and cartoons, I take
delight in them my boy and girl.
Arched over thin-leafed Herrick
and the Cavaliers. The boy
in turtleneck and khaki writes
swift notes on Marvell while he lays
one hand on her in furs beside him.
They whisper and they fill their three
by fives with data like shared sweets.
They whisper and provoke the scowls
of vestals at the long desk seated,
prim guardians of men's credos
and denials (conveyor-belted
from the caverns of Belles-Lettres).

And all the while beside me sits
this ancient, rich with muscatel,
his red face almost eyeless, the *Christian
Science Monitor* sagging from ripped knees.

- What types of sharing add to your life?
- Is it dangerous to be merely an observer of life, not a
  participant? Thank God for all the ways that you say yes to
  life.

## "View from the Window"

The view from the window, he said,
is life itself and its sheen,
at least a good quartile of it
a river, a dull-green passage, runs through yet-to-bud branches,
the river and its great ice floes
clear in the break-up of water,
and over against the green waters
a condominium stands
in clean stone, a house
that was once desolation, now
with a hundred tenants
looking out by gold lights on the river,
and, off to the west, stone terrace
up in grey lights to a skyline.

- What of life can be seen from a window?
- How does a river resemble the human journey?

# ❧ 2 ❧

# *The Gift of Creativity*

## Opening Prayer

God, you created wondrous life and saw that it was good.
Bless you for rainbows, Queen Anne's lace, babies' smiles,
arms that embrace, and visions of love. May our faith combine
with pragmatism to help cocreate new beauty, fonts of wonder.

# *Hymn*

At the new year praise the unspoken,
the scarcely conceived,
rainbows now in the making,
poems softly simmering
somewhere over the eyebrows,
murals in potency, carvings
at work in the carver,

the day is full of unbegotten,
designs not yet cut,
love before pulse beat,
palest yellow that could be sunrise.

This moment now before fleshing
lines around being,
let us praise all the potencies
under the sun.

("At the New Year")

# *God's Word*

In the beginning God created heaven and earth. Now the
earth was a formless void, there was darkness over the deep,
with a divine wind sweeping over the waters.

    God said, "Let there be light," and there was light. God
saw that light was good, and God divided light from darkness.
God called light "day," and darkness . . . "night." Evening
came and morning came: the first day. (Gen. 1:1–5)

    **Pause**: Ponder in silence the wonders of creation immedi-
ately surrounding you.

# *Reading*

It was the upward-reaching and fathomlessly hungering, heart-
breaking love for the beauty of the world at its most beautiful,
and, beyond that, for that beauty east of the sun and west of

the moon which is past the reach of all but our most desperate desiring and is finally the beauty of Beauty itself, of Being itself and what lies at the heart of Being. (Frederick Buechner, *The Sacred Journey,* p. 52)

# Canticle

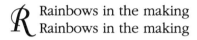 Rainbows in the making
Rainbows in the making

A marvelous chemistry of light and water
An arch on high, so fragile and free
A gift surprising the rain-filled sky
A spectrum of color to rival the peacock
A patterned dance of a summer shower

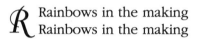 Rainbows in the making
Rainbows in the making

Praise words that simmer, becoming a poem
Praise murals in process, coming to be
Praise uncut designs and carvers' dreams
Praise love's first stirrings and unborn children
Praise seed and note, flour and glance

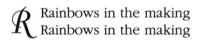 Rainbows in the making
Rainbows in the making

**Closing Prayer**

Creator God,
your divine work is in the making
and for that we praise and thank you.
Incarnate God,
you enflesh every potency
with the form of your love and life.
Redeemer,
our unspoken gratitude
yearns for expression in word and deed.
Sanctifying Spirit,
make holy our creativity

that every poem and carving and sunrise
may praise and glorify your name.
Amen. Alleluia!

# *Food for Meditation, Journaling, or Sharing*

## *Reflection*

Some summers ago, in late afternoon, a sudden rain shower
drenched our Wisconsin fields. The shower gradually subsided
just as the sun came out of hiding. The sun brought gifts, like
the Magi of old. A double rainbow filled the sky, as if reaching
from infinity to infinity. The soft and quiet colors, the smell of
the fresh rain, the warmth of a summer's day—beauty filled
the land.

Scientists provide explanations for rainbows, and for that
knowledge we should be grateful. But even the erudite and
logical propositions cannot explain the mystery of such beauty
and creativity. The best human response—silent awe. The best
praise is to imitate such magnificence by making and sharing
our own rainbows through the gift of creativity.

The painter finds his colors; the musician, her notes;
writers, their words. Gradually something from deep within—a
vision, a hope, a dream—emerges in such an attractive way as
to invite others into the landscape of beauty. When all condi-
tions are just right, oneness is experienced. Joy is felt. Creativity gives life and that rare phenomenon we call ecstasy.

Those who remain indoors do not see rainbows, nor do
they feel the moisture of the summer's rain. Those who bypass
music and poetry miss so much beauty that one wonders
about the very quality of their life. Exposure is necessary; risks
must be taken. Even though rainbows do not stay long, once
seen, their influence abides for all eternity.

## "Retrievals in Time"

It was in the folders his life lay.
In the folders his past life was resting
all through these years.
He hastened to touch the loved pages
where the verses were written
and they sprang into life like bold mornings.
He saw them as pictures, the poems taller than he—
leaves on the covered fountain—
the two hands pressed in first friendship—
the white bird out of childhood—
the pool where he swam—
liturgy lights where he and his friend prayed.

It was a retrieval of time, this reading of verses
and feeling again in his veins the joys of those mornings,
joys that would lift him again
to verse in his brave heart rising.

- Bring to mind your stories of joy and sadness—your poems.
- Praise God for the beauty retrieved in memory.
- Ask God for grace for a "brave heart rising" to meet the future creatively.

## "Integrity"

"Your story, young man, is long overdue,"
I said to him, all blackheads and hair.
Properly scowling I rapped out words,
"Turn it in tomorrow or fail."
With his short sharp look he eyed me, then
to me and to others, it seemed, he said:
"Then I fail. Maybe it's better to fail
than to turn in a nothing, words
I can run through in fifty minutes flat.
You see it's the cat. There she sits
on the steps of my story seeing all,
and the old men come and the hippies go,
but at just what point shall I make my cat
scratch on flesh what she sees and knows?"

And I sat there in wonder, flinching
under his eyes, for under the spotted
skin was something I had not learned
at his years and barely knew even now.
There are always words to play with like beads
to be strung or creation's colors to daub with,
but there was only one form, cut sharp and clear,
his one true diamond for him.
And all he could do was sit and wait
through the slow cutting of his one gem,
even though the risk was failure.

- How do you know when your time to create is upon you?
- In creating the story of your life, have you ever had to force the metaphorical cat to scratch before it was ready? How did that feel?
- What calls you forth into making something new, into giving life to your dreams and creating your rainbows?

## ❧ 3 ❧

# The Gift of Companions

### Opening Prayer

Bless you, Holy Friend, for the gift of companions—those with whom we share life. May we always be true companions, you and me and us.

# Hymn

At first it was only the stars
and the glittering constellations
that held our eyes
as we walked between snowbanks.
You, always sharper than I,
saw Orion—sword, sheath, and helmet.
The frost nipped our noses
as we looked happily skyward.

And when spring came the poets
came into vision like tall flowers rising.
You summoned them as they came to us: Frost
and Lindsay and Lowell
and Robinson, keenest of all.
I heard about Richard Cory, imperially slim,
and Luke Havergal, at western gates standing.
Sandburg we knew and broiling Chicago,
and Masters, on headstones resting.
You knew them all, my friend, my brother,
and we remember them rising,
the stars and the poets, set for our contemplation.
("First It Was Only the Stars")

# God's Word

That very same day, two of them were on their way to a
village called Emmaus, seven miles from Jerusalem, and they
were talking together about all that had happened. And it
happened that as they were talking together and discussing it,
Jesus himself came up and walked by their side; but their eyes
were prevented from recognising him. He said to them, "What
are all these things that you are discussing as you walk along?"
(Luke 24:13–17)

**Pause:** Offer a silent prayer of thanksgiving for the loyal
companions on your life's journey.

# Reading

No possession is joyous without a companion.
(Thomas Aquinas)

Above all else, it seems to me,
You need some jolly company
To see life can be fun.
(Goethe)

# Canticle

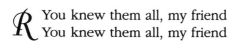 You knew them all, my friend
You knew them all, my friend

The poets came singing their songs

*William Wordsworth*
"The Child is the father of the Man;
And I could wish my days to be
Bound each to each by natural piety."

*John Donne*
"Love is a growing, or full constant light;
And his first minute, after noone, is night."

*Paul Dunbar*
"I know what the caged bird feels, alas!"

*Jessica Powers*
"God sits on a chair of darkness in my soul."

*George Herbert*
"He sweetly lived; yet sweetness did not save
His life from foes."

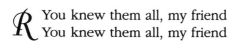 You knew them all, my friend
You knew them all, my friend

The stars arose and we call each by name

*Polaris:* hero of every longitude and latitude
*Deneb:* brightest of all the "fiery folks"
*Sirius:* barking for attention and getting it

*Regulus:* a lion of a fellow with a mighty roar

*Altair:* poised for flight into the night

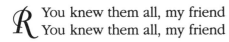 You knew them all, my friend
You knew them all, my friend

The poets raised their haunting questions:

*Christina Rossetti*
"As a tree my sin stands
To darken all lands;
Death is the fruit it bore."

*William Shakespeare*
"And yet love knows, it is a greater grief
To bear love's wrong, than hate's known injury."

*William Blake*
"Did he smile his work to see?
Did he who made the Lamb make thee?"

*Philip Sidney*
"O sweet woods, the delight of solitariness!"

*Walt Whitman*
"I harbor for good or bad, I permit to speak at every hazard,
Nature without check with original energy."

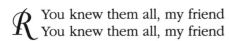 You knew them all, my friend
You knew them all, my friend

## Closing Prayer

God of snowbanks and stars and poets,
lover of beauty,
thank you for the lights of night
and the luminous poets who guide our way.
Thank you for all those who walk with us
between snowbanks, between our joys and sorrows,
between our doubts and hopes.
May we see in all companions
a sign of your providential love.
Amen. Alleluia!

# Food for Meditation, Journaling, or Sharing

## Reflection

Solitary walks often filled the days of my youth. I walked between the tracks of our country railroads that brought the Chicago Northwestern into our small village. Seldom did a companion join me, except on days that companions came to stalk wild asparagus or, as young boys are wont to do, throw stones at the glass insulators high up on the telephone poles.

Now, years and years hence, asparagus and stones have yielded to stars and poems, solitariness to companionship. With each passing season I have become increasingly aware of the importance of walking with friends who, by their very presence, double all joy and reduce by half all sorrows. They see stars I have never seen before, introduce poets (Antonio Machado, Mary Oliver, Wu-Men) who were, until then, strangers to my heart.

Walking between snowbanks or between railroad tracks can be done alone or with others. Sometimes the call is to embrace the solitary trek; other times, to join a companion or two for the sharing. Wise is the person who knows when it's winter and time to be with stars; wise too the pilgrim who, in spring, joins the poets to hear them sing.

## "For Joseph My Brother"

It is out of guilt that words come,
the free flowing words of my song of regret
for not fully loving the man
to whom I have owed everything,
all that I prize, the gifts
that made life worth living.

I think of the pages we turned, the classic pages,
the long winter evenings when side by side
we read out Dickens and enjoyed the Pickwickian revels.
I think of the lakeshore, the concert,
the *Egmont Overture* lifting us to new wonder.

You ever first, the leader, opening archways
to art and music and letters,
and I the follower, never fully loving
you and your volume of gifts.
Now let me offer my praise and remembrance
to you, my gracious departed,
my on-living brother.

- Who have been your companions into the worlds of art, music, letters, or other worlds that have given inspiration to your life? How have you thanked these companions for their gift?
- Is there any relationship about which you have guilt or regrets? Can you still mend the relationship? Pray for the graces you need to be a true companion.

## "Brother Fidelis Remembered"

We learned in this room that joy is supple
and flowing, that it opens a door
and tall, commanding, and restless,
improvises a lesson
with sudden shifts and sharp reversals.

We learned that joy is black and lithe, that grace
of motion is the language of power,
that joy is a sinuous thing,
never resting but catching hold
of men, winding its music round them.

In this room that has been for long
to dullness dedicated,
there was a new and wondrous thing,
the sound of men responding
to tall, imperious joy.

- Ponder how companions have brought you to joy?
- Who have been your mentors "to tall, imperious joy"? Thank God for them.
- Sing a hymn of joy that sums up the gifts of companions.

## ❧ 4 ❧

# The Gift of Music

### Opening Prayer

God, you are the music of the spheres. Help us hear you and be swept up in the harmony and passion of you. We praise you with glad sounds and joyous voices.

# Hymn

She knew that once she had lit
the candles, drawn the drapes,
and set the needle to the disk,
she could lie back in grandeur listening
to her kings: the one her Celt
in mask and emerald cloak, singing long
and artfully to a listless world,
the other her south German, brooding
among his firs and statues,
setting the night to music, making it rise
and grow with his massed delicacy.
These were her kings and this their sovereign
magic, clothing her sparse room
in apocalyptic hangings, their
rich prophet voices lifting her
to heady glee above the tea
and candles to where the poets sit
with Wisdom playing before the world.

("Magic at Night")

# God's Word

Sing out in praise of God our strength,
acclaim the God of Jacob and Rachel.
Take pipe and timbrel;
take tuneful harp and lyre.
Blow the trumpet for the new month,
for the full moon on the day of our pilgrim-feast.

(Ps. 81:1–3, *Psalms Anew*)

Sing a new song to Yahweh,
who has done wonderful deeds,

. . . . . . . . . . .

Sing praise to Yahweh all the earth;
ring out your joy.

(Ps. 98:1–4, *Psalms Anew*)

**Pause**: Listen to a piece of your favorite music; play or sing in glory to God.

# Reading

We are born and grow up with a fondness for each other, and we have genes for that. We can be talked out of it, for the genetic message is like a distant music and some of us are hard-of-hearing. Societies are noisy affairs, drowning out the sound of ourselves and our connection. Hard-of-hearing, we go to war. Stone-deaf, we make thermonuclear missiles. Nonetheless, the music is there, waiting for more listeners. (Lewis Thomas, *Late Night Thoughts on Listening to Mahler's Ninth Symphony*, p. 105)

# Canticle

℟ Setting the night to music
Setting the night to music

Song: making a light shine in the darkness
Aria: turning dullness of life into glory
Concerto: pulling the soul into ecstasy
Cadenza: challenging the flight of a windhover
Hymn: lifting time into eternity

℟ Setting the night to music
Setting the night to music

Violin: an ocean of sound ebbing and flowing
Drum: a human heartbeat felt by all
Trumpet: an arrow piercing the depth of the soul
Oboe: a haunting owl stirring hidden melancholy
Piccolo: a hummingbird seeking a place to rest

℟ Setting the night to music
Setting the night to music

**Closing Prayer**

God of song and dance,
our nights are long and lonely,
fill them with the magic of music
that we know how to do the dance of life
and bring light to a weary world.
Amen. Alleluia!

# *Food for Meditation, Journaling, or Sharing*

## *Reflection*

Only one word can convey the quality of the tone: mellow. The high school senior played the "Trumpeter's Lullaby" at the Christmas concert. I was only a freshman and attended the concert through the sufferance of my older sister and her boyfriend. Like most of the audience, I knew little about music, but we basked in the mellow tones emanating from this golden horn glittering in the spotlight.

Music has an affinity with the soul. It's a natural environment, like water for fish. Without music, the journey is diminished—sometimes unto death. The body can continue to function and move about, but vitality eludes us. A spiritual vacuum seems to open up. Music enriches the soul by means of osmosis.

## *"Mozart in Motion"*

He would have loved it,
the sweep of an adagio
over green hills,
an andante rolling
out smoothly
to a far cloud bank.

Violins sing within wheels.
Clarinets brave the west wind
for a clear bounding.

Trees and hedges are caught
in a swift cadenza.

He would have loved it
and laughed to hear it,
his own bright music
loosed on the land,
music held and contained
but by a closure of trees.

- Listen to a favorite instrumental piece and allow yourself to
  be swept into nature. Praise God for music playing through
  your imagination.
- Go outside. Walk mindfully along and listen to the natural
  music of tree and wind, bird and insect.

## "Concerto 21"

This music bids us memorize
our rooms and gardens, lightly,
gravely touch our doors and windows,
look farewell upon the tiger lily
and white rose.

This music is a taking leave
of order, lays light hands
on fountains and statues,
softly, solemnly invokes
God's sculptured hands.

These measures are forewarning
(and those lips, two hundred years in dust):
Hold them close, the glass, the flower,
the cluster. Hold them close
and memorize them well,
for even now you hear far off
the footfalls, the destroyer,
and the end of order.

- Listen to music that bids you to memorize the gifts you
  enjoy in life and invokes "God's sculptured hands."
- Can music help you accept your own passing as part of the
  harmony of life? Talk with the loving God about this.

# ❧ 5 ❧

# *The Gift of Poetry*

## Opening Prayer

Word Made Flesh, your life is pure poetry. While what poets write reflects only a portion of your divine harmony, may I pluck goodness and beauty from it. May I attend to the best poetry, "what man's soul experiences when he is listening to his inner song, a song that has no words" (Felix Marti-Ibañez, *The Crystal Arrow,* p. xv).

# Hymn

A tree, like an idea, stands straight and tall.
I at the upper window was struck by it
as by a sudden resolve to make a great poem
standing erect in beauty,
perpendicular, thrusting into the world.
I know that the tree was maple and its gifts were golden.
It stood there flaunting its gold,
giving itself, needlessly generous
to all with the wit to know and to love it,
just as I, gratuitous poet,
would rustle my leaves, my poems,
for all with the wit and desire
to see and to hear them.

("A Tree Like an Idea")

# God's Word

—I am the rose of Sharon,
the lily of the valleys.

—As a lily among the thistles,
so is my beloved among girls.

—As an apple tree among the trees of the wood,
so is my love among young men.
In his delightful shade I sit,
and his fruit is sweet to my taste.
He has taken me to his cellar,
and his banner over me is love.

(Song of Songs 2:1–4)

**Pause**: Be still and invite God's Spirit to speak through
your inner voice.

# Reading

Somewhere between the minute particular and the essence lies the land of poetry. (May Sarton, *Journal of a Solitude,* p. 97)

How is it that the poets have said so many fine things about our first love, so few about our later love? Are their first poems their best? Or are not those the best which come from their fuller thought, their larger experience, their deeper-rooted affections? The boy's flutelike voice has its own spring charm; but the man should yield a richer deeper music. (George Eliot, *Adam Bede,* p. 475)

# Canticle

 Would rustle my leaves, my poems
Would rustle my leaves, my poems

Maple leaves, golden and holy
Oak leaves, brown and strong
Ash leaves, gray and shimmering
Birch leaves, yellow and friendly
Cherry leaves, crimson and warm

 Would rustle my leaves, my poems
Would rustle my leaves, my poems

Love poems, matters of the heart
Nature poems, matters of the earth
Religious poems, matters of the soul
Dark poems, matters of the night
Question poems, matters of the quest

 Would rustle my leaves, my poems
Would rustle my leaves, my poems

**Closing Prayer**

God of trees and poems,
all creation is a rustle of your love,
all life, a poetic expression of your goodness.

Teach us, with wit and desire, to know you, gratuitous Poet,
and to see and hear your marvelous works and words.
May we stand erect in beauty
and resolve to make a great poem of our life.
Amen. Alleluia!

# *Food for Meditation, Journaling, or Sharing*

## *Reflection*

In the autumn of 1958, during my second year of college, I took a literature class that emphasized poetry. The class and the teacher altered my life.

Our teacher was demanding, competent, and knowledgeable. He required that we memorize poems and regularly recite them in class.

Becoming intimate with poems opened a door into a new world and a pantheon of great figures: Rilke, Shakespeare, Milton, Dickinson, and Blake. Here were people gifted with special insight into the human condition and skilled in literary expression. Their shared gift made life more radiant, a better place. Their verses enlarged the heart and stirred the soul.

Poetry is a moment—sometimes minor, sometimes major—of ecstasy. It lifts us above the humdrum into the realm of vision or courage or simple joy. But a Chinese proverb reminds us, "After the ecstasy, go do the laundry." Most of life is laundry, ordinary and common duty. Nevertheless, ecstasy, poetry, and transcendence have their rightful place. A memorized poem reminds us of this fact and, when recited during laundry, anoints that work—all work—with a special grace.

## *"After My Silent Summer"*

After my silent summer
the words fall out of broad branches.
Where they come from I cannot guess.
I have sat and idled under the leaves
hearing the twitter of coveys of women.

I have taken white wine, but the words,
hanging there as the breeze touched,
did not come to me as I idled
under the sun.

After the passage of women
and the long shadows and chiming
of voices, after footsteps
of students and strollers and patter of children,
suddenly, but in full time, the words fall
and I gather them, one by one, smiling.

- Rest in silence and bring to mind some concrete image, symbol, or metaphor that summarizes God's love in your life—a garden, light, the sunrise, a lily—anything that represents for you the abiding love of God. In your imagination experience the image—its sounds, tastes, textures, smells, and sight. Let the feelings that surround this image rise up within you and draw you to an even deeper love of God.
- Write a psalm, which means "song," that pours out your feelings right now. Hold nothing back—anger, sorrow, joy, or thanksgiving. God already knows what is in your heart. Writing helps you share who you are with God, your holy and true friend.

## "Suburban Night"

And I must sit here as the cousins
patter, sit and rock my soul
and know there is no issue from this night.
For this was I born, to hear
how lawns are seeded, hedges clipped,
and babies bathed, to sip my gin
and feel the mean words wash against me,
wishwash of the enclosed
suburban night.

Somewhere outside this padded room,
beyond this stucco and the two
thin trees that guard it
men are speaking of the long
and swaying lines of freedom,

men are mellowing out the night hours
with cordials of Rilke and of Yeats,
but I was born to hear the cousins
patter and be taught the virtues
of varnish and of seal.

- Find some poetry to read. If you have not touched this potent brew for a long time, look for some Frost, Dickinson, Robinson, or even Sandburg. Or ponder the Psalms. Open your heart and mind to poems, stairs to the inner life.
- Write a haiku. These little poems express a striking image that has somehow touched us. Typically a haiku helps us see an image in a new way. In English, haiku are written in three lines. Here are two examples:

  A black bear pawing
  Fast-moving gray clouds, thunder
  storms the apple tree.

  Squawking magpie
  scolds the shadowed mesa
  from the barbed wire fence.

Creation itself and the experience of creation magnify God's work. Look at what is around you here and now that speaks of God's goodness to you. Write about what you see.

❧    ❧    ❧

# *Mystery*

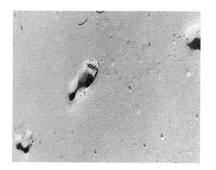

## ❧ 6 ❧

# The Mystery of Nature

**Opening Prayer**

You constantly surprise us, creator God, with the mystery of
nature. Seasons change, leaving us in wonder at the twists
and turns of our life. May we keep our senses open to signs
of you, and to the lessons you teach through gray storms and
dreamy blue skies, spring greenness and winter whiteness.

# Hymn

Why do we fear the snow
and the seethe of it over the cities,
as though its white was leprous,
a sign of death on the skyline?
The frail old men go fearing
the ice glaze on the pavement.
The motorist on the freeway
fears flurries and sudden blindness,
and the timorous keep to their houses
as the snow drifts deep at the door.

We take this first night of winter
remembering how we once danced in it,
rolled in it, sledded its ghostly
inclines, leaving us laughing
and freshened, like creatures baptized
in winter's first glory, waiting
to see on the windows the sign,
not of death but of magic.

(“Fear of Snow”)

# God's Word

You [God] set springs gushing in ravines,
flowing between the mountains,
giving drink to wild animals,
drawing the thirsty wild donkeys.
The birds of the air make their nests
and sing among the branches nearby.

· · · · · · · · · · · ·

Yahweh, how many are the works you have created,
arranging everything in wisdom!
Earth is filled with creatures you have made:
see the vast ocean
teeming with countless creatures, great and small,
where ships go to and fro,
and Leviathan that made to play for you.

· · · · · · · · · · · ·

Glory forever to you, Yahweh!
May you find joy in your creation.
(Ps. 104:10–12,24–26,31, *Psalms Anew*)

**Pause**: Bring to your mind a favorite place in nature: at the seashore, up in the hills, by a stream. Bless the Creator.

# Reading

The best remedy for those who are afraid, lonely, or unhappy is to go outside, somewhere where they can be quite alone with the heavens, nature, and God. Because only then does one feel that all is as it should be and that God wishes to see people happy, amidst the simple beauty of nature. As long as this exists, and it certainly always will, I know that then there will always be comfort for every sorrow, whatever the circumstances may be. And I firmly believe that nature brings solace in all troubles. (B. M. Mooyaart-Doubleday, trans., *Anne Frank*, p. 172)

# Canticle

R The snow drifts deep at the door
  The snow drifts deep at the door

Is it death or magic that we see?
Is ice always an enemy and a foe?
Is winter baptism felt behind closed doors?
Is the leprosy of whiteness curable?
Is winter's first night also a first glory?

R The snow drifts deep at the door
  The snow drifts deep at the door

And children sculpt coal-eyed snowpeople
And teachers rejoice at the gift of a snow day
And plow drivers curse the blinding blizzard
And deer dread the days of famine
And weather predictions come true

*R* The snow drifts deep at the door
The snow drifts deep at the door

**Closing Prayer**

God of snow and rain,
of sun and moon,
we fragile human creatures are subject to the elements.
May we rejoice in their beauty, respect their power.
Though we struggle to see your providence
in nature's massive indiscriminate indifference,
help us to be faithful to your call,
in and out of season,
in and out of every storm.
Amen. Alleluia!

# *Food for Meditation, Journaling, or Sharing*

## *Reflection*

The Sullivan farm lay three miles west of our village. During my grade school years, I visited there often. Winter was a favorite time. The snow had free play in the open fields, and drifts of great diversity, like early homesteaders, took up residence where they willed. Drifts proved a white-golden opportunity for making midwestern igloos.

In those days before television, we children were forced out of doors to find things to do. Despite the cold and bitter winds, play and unselfconscious fellowship warmed our hearts and bodies. The whiteness of the rural landscape became part of our inner geography, never to be forgotten. A treasured section of life would be missing were the snowdrifts deep at the door taken from our stories.

Snow taught us many lessons, especially when it came with extravagance and played its game of tag with the wind. Lesson 1: Snow is ubiquitously impartial. Rich and poor, well and sick, learned and uneducated—all received equal treatment. Lesson 2: Beauty and terror can go together. Our blizzards, the drift creators, startled us with their beauty while shocking us with their power. People perished because the doors to safety were drifted over. Lesson 3: Snow spontaneously propels children into play. The awesome freedom of snow seemed to yell in our minds: "Find your skis, sled, boots. Come and play. Join in the dance of life!"

What would life be like in a climate bereft of the crunch of snow underfoot, the fanciful sculptures of snowdrifts, the soft hush of feathery flakes! It's hard to imagine. Even in our imagination, "stopping by woods on a snowy evening" offers a deep richness.

## "Fallen Leaves"

Fallen leaves without number, a broad field of them,
taking the sun of October,
orange and gold, copper and brown, and all the shades of
redness,
they feel the breeze flutter them
glorious on grass
in a kind of triumph of color
under the dull-penciled city.

I stoop to the leaves and swish them,
in love with their fallen glory here by the freeway,
and I think of the bodies, the flesh and bone of the bodies
of men cut down by oppressors,
and I think of the splendid bodies
of young men under the sun,
mowed down and left to waste
like the fallen leaves of October.

- Ponder the glory of fall by going out and attending to it or, if you are in the midst of another season, going inside and attending to it in your imagination.
- Fall is a time to touch our grief—that strange mixture of splendor and sadness. If you have untended grieving to do, invite Jesus or another wisdom figure to sit with you to grieve and let go.

## "Spring Song" (To end all spring songs)

Now that the earth has shed
its white thermal winter wear,
spring is upon us. Sometimes I fear
the sting and smell of it, dust
in the eyes, change in the blood.
(At the library window I stand
with checked papers, one hand
on the sill, feeling the sun).
Spring is puddles for boots
to slosh through, puddles reflecting
a cloud, a tree, a Chevelle.
Spring is the lift of the heart when we pass
open bars where the new beer
foams on the lips of the dreamers.
Spring means sassafras gum
we chew for tired bowels, bitter cucumbers,
lettuce fresh from the garden, the green
that is almost gold on the bushes.

Spring has come singing off-key
its needless music. How much better
it was to sleep in winter snugness
and forget them: the pools, the little green leaves,
the white blossoms, the boys and girls
on wheels, let loose on creation.

- Does spring really have a somber side as the poem sug-
  gests? Or should we just sing to the cycle of nature and
  dance to the fecundity of the earth?
- Make a poem-list of your favorite spring images. Pray it as a
  song of joy to God.

## ✸ 7 ✸

# The Mystery of God

**Opening Prayer**

God, you show us any face that will lure us into love with you: mother, father, wisdom, creator, Jesus, Spirit, and so many more. Praise to you, God who is always mystery, but always wishes to be known.

# *Hymn*

God is not nice.
Frankly I would think twice
before inviting him to tea.
He would bore us with long silences
and sit and crumble cake
and eye us owlishly.

I am sure I would be hard pressed
before I would make a house guest
of this king. He would untidy
my chaste rooms with sudden
gusts of grandeur, and I would be picking up
all day after the Almighty.

In truth I would become delirious
living with this imperious
Lover. He would rip the fine design
I have stitched for my pleasant days,
saying, "I must be rude
if I am to be divine."

("God Is Not Nice")

# *God's Word*

How profound are the riches, the wisdom, and the knowledge of God. How mysterious and incomprehensible are God's ways. Who has known the mind of God? Who has tried to counsel God or been able to give God anything and earn something in return. From God, through God, and for God all things have their existence. Glory to God forever and ever. Amen. (Adapted from Rom. 11:33–36)

**Pause**: Ponder your questions about God.

# Reading

In 1925, Evelyn Underhill wrote: "Now the experience of God . . . is, I believe, in the long run always a vocational experience. It always impels to some sort of service: always awakens an energetic love. It never leaves the self where it found it." (Dana Greene, *Evelyn Underhill,* p. 98)

What do I owe, who hold my God to be not only the generous Giver of my life, its beneficent Governor, its holy Comforter, its careful Director, and above all these its most liberal Redeemer, everlasting Protector, Defender, Glorifier. (G. R. Evans, trans., *Bernard of Clairvaux,* p. 185)

# Canticle

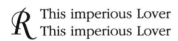 This imperious Lover
This imperious Lover

Whose rudeness brings all grace
Whose silence fills our emptiness
Whose gusts of grandeur cleanse our hearts
Whose owlish eyes bring sudden joy
Whose un-nicety is so gracious

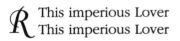 This imperious Lover
This imperious Lover

Invited everyday for tea and crumpets
Pressed hard to become our sovereign guest
Pursued in tidiness as recorder of our days
Overheard telling of divine surprises
Content with peace-filled silences

℞ This imperious Lover
This imperious Lover

### Closing Prayer

Wisdom,
break our every attempt to dominate you.
Give us wisdom to know you in the breaking of our heart
and in the strange visitations of your Spirit.
May we experience that holy, delirious loving that comes
with your gracious rudeness.
Amen. Alleluia!

# Food for Meditation, Journaling, or Sharing

## Reflection

Adjectives color our life and thereby help us to know the identity of the world that surrounds us, even the world that inhabits us. Would we recognize an apple if it were not red, a pumpkin if it were not orange, a blue jay if it did not match the sky? And how do we recognize God without adjectives to set divinity apart from "creatureliness." The bold poets attempt their color theology by modifying God through the use of adjectives.

Francis Thompson, in his famous poem "The Hound of Heaven," writes of God:

I said to Dawn: Be sudden—to Eve: Be soon;
    With thy young skiey blossoms heap me over
        From this tremendous Lover.

One senses the extravagance of God here. Frugality never resided in the heavenly courts. The divine economy is one of abundance without waste, generosity without condescension, and affluence without self-consciousness. Divine love is ultimately simple in its magnificence. Thompson's explosive "tremendous" captures only a small segment of such vast mystery.

My friend Brother Edward calls God rude. God's almighty love can seem imperious, but such an accusation is probably a psychological projection. Brother Edward might be laughing at his secret joke—the paradox and mystery of God's imperious or rude love.

God appears as a hound when our life is wild, and we need to be chased home. God appears imperious when we are arrogant, overbearing, and dictatorial with others—including God. God appears angry when our own sin and darkness blot out the light and freeze all. The wild, the arrogant, and the prodigal seldom find inviting God over for tea very pleasant.

## "The Strange One"

This Lord of ours is a strange one.
He throws out hints
on our little landscape, flicking
our fields with his frost,
letting us know the soft rains
have passed and the seagulls.

Here in the pheasant season
he cuts a fine figure in trees
all but stripped, and only his chosen
know that this skeletal world
is the fairest of all.

Now before snow the silencer
shifts through the trees,
now before death the white beauty
sits on the hills,
"Take the day," says the strange one,
"and stand as my trees stand,
watching."

- What hints of God's presence are flicked in your path every day? Be especially conscious of the little ones. Thank God as you meet them.
- Talk with God about times when God has seemed particularly strange.

## "Presence"

It is above, below, and around me,
a prevailing presence, like sunlight
on birds flying upward.

The voice is a presence, the eyes
as they enter me speaking their mercy.
At the table he sits inclined to me
hearing my hope and my desperation.
Somehow he has entered me,
this teacher, this healer of bodies.

His presence is more than secret coming.
It colors the room where we rest.
It freshens the breeze from the window.
It seems it is life itself,
sacred life mounting my spirit.

- Ponder and then praise God in light, in eyes that have touched your soul in moments of healing.
- Create a mandala, a symbolic picture, of your relationship with God right now. Use colors and objects that speak to the feelings of the relationship.

## ❦ 8 ❦

# *The Mystery of Suffering*

### Opening Prayer

My God, my God, I often feel that you have abandoned me to
suffering. Be with me even by recognizing your absence.
Guide me somehow through suffering to deeper sensitivity,
greater love, and firm hope.

# Hymn

You will never be as alone as now
in the sudden flare and stab of it
there in your side where the ribs sit.
You live in the strictest privacy
you will ever be knowing.
No hand can soothe, no mind can reach
the darkened cage where you toss.
The stabs are staggered. You never know
the exact time of the knife.
You have learned too well that your pain
is yours, inalienably yours.
This evil you have learned to claim
as yours, undeniably yours.
Even as a harassed father must claim
his basest child and most hideous.

("Pain")

# God's Word

They came to a plot of land called Gethsemane, and [Jesus]
said to his disciples, "Stay here while I pray." Then he took
Peter and James and John with him. And he began to feel
terror and anguish. And he said to them, "My soul is sorrowful
to the point of death. Wait here, and stay awake." And going
on a little further he threw himself on the ground and prayed
that, if it were possible, this hour might pass him by. "Abba,
Father!" he said, "For you everything is possible. Take this cup
away from me. But let it be as you, not I, would have it."
(Mark 14:32–36)

**Pause:** What suffering—what cup—would you want God
to remove from you?

# Reading

For suffering smashes to pieces the complacency of our normal fictions about reality, and forces us to become alive in a special sense—to see carefully, to feel deeply, to touch ourselves and our worlds in ways we have heretofore avoided. It has been said, and truly I think, that suffering is the first grace. In a special sense, suffering is almost a time of rejoicing, for it marks the birth of creative insight. (Ken Wilber, *No Boundary*, p. 85)

If it is only at the centre of our being that suffering is resolved, is it not there that we are nearest God? Is it even the road to [God] if we knew how to travel it? (Florida Scott-Maxwell, *The Measure of My Days*, p. 84)

# Canticle

℟ The exact time of the knife
The exact time of the knife

Winter, the stab of the icicle piercing the snow
Spring, the stab of the violet struggling for light
Summer, the stab of the sun blinding the eyes
Autumn, the stab of the geese announcing the cold

℟ The exact time of the knife
The exact time of the knife

Dawn, the knife of youth's foolish hopes
Noon, the knife of complacent maturity
Dusk, the knife of midlife regrets
Midnight, the knife of the last loneliness

℟ The exact time of the knife
The exact time of the knife

**Closing Prayer**

God with us,
you claim us as your children, in our beauty and baseness;
you are present with us always,
whether we are humble or hideous.
Help us to understand the theology of the knife,
the terrible mystery of suffering and pain.
Grant us compassion for our hurting sisters and brothers.
Through your Son's Passion make all pain redemptive.
Amen. Alleluia!

# *Food for Meditation, Journaling, or Sharing*

## *Reflection*

Going barefoot in summer, however unhygienic, was one of the pleasures of growing up in a rural village. At least once a summer that pleasure turned in a wink to sharp pain. Unprotected by canvas or leather, our toes would smack a piece of raised concrete or ram into a door that opened unexpectedly. The scream, the blood, the tears, and the hurrying home for healing and consolation.

Stubbed toes, broken hearts fill life: the midnight call that one's child has been killed in a car accident; the doctor's announcement that a spouse has six months to live; the severed relationship; the shock of being nakedly alone; the stab of conscience at the recognition of sin.

Suffering has the quality of solitude. Even though family and friends may be near at hand, our suffering is our own. It bears our fingerprints, is seared with our brand. Empathy often seems to only intensify the pain. So we attempt to suffer in silence as we have been told to do all along.

The paradox of pain dwells in its possible redemptive power. It can goad us to authenticity. It can slice away whatever is extraneous, pretentious, illusory. It shatters romanticism. So some poets pray for suffering, John Donne, for example:

Batter my heart, three person'd God, for, you
As yct but knocke, breathe, shine, and seeke to mend;
That I may rise, and stand, o'erthrow mee, 'and bend
Your force to breake, blowe, burn and make me new.
(*The Divine Poems,* p. 11)

Even though we do not know the exact time of the knife, we can come to know the grace of pain's paradox. It can make all things new!

## "A Young Man Stooping"

There were always the flowers
and the old man loved them, the breeze
blowing gray locks as he stooped.
God, it seemed, had moved far from him,
and the men he lived with
turned their backs and cruised onward.
He loved them all—the marigolds, the geraniums,
the strange spider flowers, and his own gladioli,
one of them shooting up bravely brilliant yellow
straight up to his shoulders.
And suddenly there was a shadow, a very long shadow
over him and the flower beds.
He looked up and saw blue jeans,
sleeveless shirt, and broad shoulders,
at least six feet of it all, the eyes
meeting his own in pleased wonder.

"I never saw them so tall, the gladioli I mean,"
he said and stooped downward.
The young man spoke with almost reverent delight.
Never had men looked at flowers and touched so.
The old man looked into his eyes and loved him.
How strange it was that when God and men had shunned him,
this young man should stand, a sign of wonder,
with whom he could speak
as though he had always known him.

- Recall times when you have felt shunned, lonely? Who or what was your "young man"? Ponder the mystery and gladness of these redemptive moments.

- To whom do you come as the "young man" to bring joy and wonder? Thank God for the opportunity to help others see the flowers.

## "All Through the Loneliness"

All through the loneliness of midday to dusk
he at the train window sat looking out
on snow-filled furrows repeating, repeating
waves of silence on covered fields,
and out of the furrows a woman's hand
was stretching out in its violet sleeve to him,
a withered hand, a sacramental
freshness he had touched.

Her presence moved over windmills,
frozen streams, and little leafless trees.
An off-white world was lifted
to her stooped and gentle greatness.
She the aged woman he had kissed
the morning of this longest day
had made herself eternal
with the song that tolled within,
with the snow-filled furrows on the land.

- Who sings within you to lure you into life and out of loneliness? Praise God for the song.
- If you need to grieve the passing of a loved one or some other part of your life, say your lamentation to God and, if possible, to a small group of understanding friends. Tell the stories; let yourself laugh and cry. Then through some ritual act, ask God to help you let go.

# ❧ 9 ❧

# The Mystery of Death

### Opening Prayer

Eternal God, you do not give death the last word. With you, death is only a dance into new life. May my dance be a soothing waltz or a happy tango.

# Hymn

Let death, luminous death,
let death divest the darkness
and let the light shine forth
so that we can see more clearly the aging dancers
performing there against mercy's backdrops,
dancers who show their grace
in bending and stooping and raising other men upward.
They are God's dancers who show their powers
with pointer and chalk and design,
with lens and light and screen
as they lift men upward to see
figures of unknown Godhead.

The dancers have fallen,
and the God who has loved them has raised them
to dance after death,
where walls without end mirror their perfect bodies.
They leap and they lunge,
they pause and sweep on, those perfect bodies,
and it seems they are beckoning us upward
to them, to luminous death,
and to dance after death and the darkness.

("Death, Luminous Death,"
to the memory of Brothers Alphonsus and Vincent)

# God's Word

Jesus told Martha:
I am the resurrection.
Anyone who believes in me, even though that person dies,
    will live,
and whoever lives and believes in me
will never die.

(John 11:25–26)

**Pause**: Ask yourself, Do I feel that death is luminous and divests the darkness?

# Reading

"Of course [death] means you are going away from us for good," she said with a sigh. "But that don't mean I'll lose you. Look at my papa here; he's been dead all these years, and yet he is more real to me than almost anybody else. He never goes out of my life. I talk to him and consult him all the time. The older I grow, the better I know him and the more I understand him." (Willa Cather, *My Antonia,* p. 362)

# Canticle

 After death and the darkness
After death and the darkness

Light to make all shadows luminous
Light to dispel all fear of darkness
Light to warm the hearts of friends and foes
Light to guide us into the new country
Light to bring joy in the morning and evening

 After death and the darkness
After death and the darkness

Mercy that wipes away all blame
Mercy that reveals God's forgiving heart
Mercy that ends all shame and guilt
Mercy that unites people in majestic solidarity
Mercy that frees us to know our true self

 After death and the darkness
After death and the darkness

Dance with all the angels and saints
Dance with the lion and the lamb
Dance with the hills and the mountains
Dance with the stars and the clouds
Dance with friends and all loved ones

 After death and the darkness
After death and the darkness

**Closing Prayer**

God of light,
help us always to see your loving kindness.
God of mercy,
draw us into your forgiving embrace.
God of the dance,
may we rejoice in your holy will.
We fear darkness and death.
We ask for the grace of trust
that all fears may cease
and our heart may be free,
even before death and darkness, to praise thee.
Amen. Alleluia!

# *Food for Meditation,*
# *Journaling, or Sharing*

## *Reflection*

On the retreat houseboat Quo Vadis, crossing from the main-
land to Chambers Island (approximately a five-mile trip), four
young lads caught a ride. Classmates and musicians, they were
sharing a minor adventure during the summer between their
sophomore and junior years of high school. Before one
o'clock the next afternoon, one of the boys had drowned off
South Point.

When death comes to our elders we are somewhat
prepared. Not so when an entire life lies before a youth filled
with talent, energy, and enthusiasm. The tragic drowning took
my breath away. The untimely death shocked all the retreat-
ants who were themselves searching out the meaning of life.

Like the ocean or the galaxy, death and life are mysteries
so immense and incomprehensible that they leave us awe-
struck. We can handle a stream, but not the Pacific; a star on
the Christmas tree, but not Orion. We flounder when confront-
ed by the mystery of existence.

I did not know the boy who drowned, our only encounter was a brief glance. Nonetheless, that solitary moment,
that simple glance, will never leave me. Within twenty-four
hours, that bursting energy and dream of a wonderful future
vanished, leaving pain and grief.

Death comes not only for the archbishop but for us all.
The bell tolls for king and serf, old and young, individuals and
societies. Death can paralyze us, but it need not. Before its
dying, each day offers the opportunity to live life to its fullest.
The choice is ours.

## "At the Airport"

It was easy to phrase compassion over the clouds,
the sun in the rolls of them, gold and rose in their depths,
but as my heart dipped down, down with the engines,
and under the clouds I saw the trees and the rooftops coming.
I felt panic flaring over compassion
and in my throat the words choked,
soft, safe words, words couching compassion.
What would I say to the stricken man
waiting there at the gate?
Unbuckled, now moving, I made my way down the rampway.
In the eddy of heads there by the post was the gaunt one.
I stepped forward. I grasped his hand cautiously,
saying, after all efforts at phrasing,
"Jim, I know how you feel, how hard it's been."
He pulled back his hand, the widowed man in white anger.
"What do you mean you know how I feel?
How can you? I've been through hell.
You've never been there nor will be."
Ashamed and aghast, I stood there
and saw my gaunt brother weeping.

* What do you say in the face of death's loss?
* Is compassion always so inadequate in response to those
  stricken by grief?
* Talk with Jesus about how he dealt with the mystery of
  death and all the feelings that emerged with it.

## "The Dead"

They are around us, irrepressibly round us,
the gentle and not so gentle,
sometimes quite near, like mice
in the wastebasket skittering,
sometimes like soughs of distant
waters washing against the city,
not only at night, when they tap
child-fingered against the pane,
but at the surfeit of dinner when talk drowses down,
we look around, they are there
whispering their piquant secrets.

We are an island; they, many billioned,
spread in small waves around us,
a sea unmeasured and tideless which laps
against our barriers, gently eroding
them, lapping and quietly taking.

- Who are some of the dead who skitter or sough into your consciousness reassuringly, gently, affirmingly? Pray with them; be with them.
- Are there any among the dead whose presence frightens, challenges, or disturbs you? Reflect on why and how. Then be with them. Seek peace and let go.
- Talk with God about your own passing over. Offer your own psalm of death.

## ∾ 10 ∾

# The Mystery of Resurrection

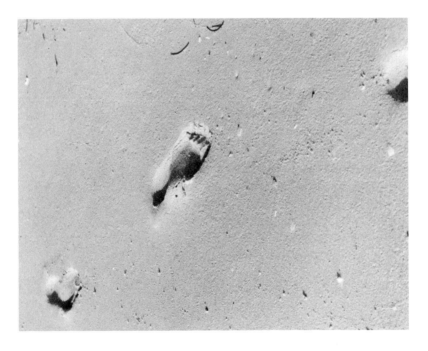

**Opening Prayer**

Living God, your Son's Resurrection deposed death's reign over humanity. May we take heart and truly live in this knowledge.

# Hymn

No eye has seen
the bodies, the brave and lustrous bodies
walking superb
among golden branches, seen the horses,
winged and scarlet mounts,
waiting to take the eternal riders,
swift as starfire, there beside the sea
whose breakers rise to touch the constellations.

Nor ear heard
the contrapuntal lights aloft
the glistening orchards or heard fingers play
on strings all strung across
white gardens where the lovers stroll,
nor heard the voices of men statuesque
scaling circular stairs,
music as deep as love,
taller than expectation.

Nor has it entered the heart of man
how men and women, contemplative
of one another, touch and know
how love can rise, a mounting wave
within them, and their eyes
can never surfeit on each other's beauty,
while the great world, love itself,
lifts and transports them in compulsive motion.

("No Eye Has Seen")

# God's Word

After this perishable nature has put on imperishability and this mortal nature has put on immortality, then will the words of scripture come true: Death is swallowed up in victory. Death, where is your victory? Death, where is your sting? The sting of death is sin, and the power of sin comes from the Law. Thank God, then, for giving us the victory through Jesus Christ. . . .

So, . . . keep firm and immovable, always abounding in energy for [God's] work, being sure that in [God] none of your labours is wasted. (1 Cor. 15:54–58)

**Pause**: Ponder this question: Do I really believe that death is swallowed up in the victory of Christ?

# Reading

My understanding was lifted up into heaven, where I saw our Lord God as a lord in his own house, who has called all his friends to a splendid feast. . . . I saw him reign in his house as a king and fill it all full of joy and mirth, gladdening and consoling his dear friends with himself, very familiarly and courteously, with wonderful melody in endless love in his own fair blissful countenance, which glorious countenance fills all heaven full of the joy and bliss of the divinity. (Edmund Colledge and James Walsh, trans., *Julian of Norwich*, p. 203)

# Canticle

℟ Resurrection, gardens where the lovers stroll
 Resurrection, gardens where the lovers stroll

Adam, naming creation that first week
Eve, making a home between the great rivers
Mary Magdalene, searching for her Savior
Peter, James, and John, fighting off fear and sleep
Jesus, embracing God's will for him

℟ Resurrection, gardens where the lovers stroll
 Resurrection, gardens where the lovers stroll

Andalusia, Spain's garden of music, dance, and love
Amboise, France's garden of flowers, wine, and joy
Thurgau, Switzerland's garden of precision, mountains, and
      hope
Carlow, Ireland's garden of tales, songs, and leprechauns
Kent, England's garden of cricket, trees, and endless paths

R Resurrection, gardens where the lovers stroll
  Resurrection, gardens where the lovers stroll

**Closing Prayer**

In the cool of the evening, gracious God,
you stroll through creation,
looking for those who love and who tend your garden well.
From whatever land we come from,
call us to be your companions.
You have entrusted your garden of life to us.
We praise you for this confidence;
we thank you for this mission;
we beseech you to walk with us always,
until the final resurrection.
Amen. Alleluia!

# *Food for Meditation, Journaling, or Sharing*

## *Reflection*

In the Chronicles of Narnia, C. S. Lewis uses the image of Shadow-Lands to give us a glimpse of the relationship between our temporal existence and the afterlife. Now we live in shadows, but with death we leave the shadows and enter into the fullness of light and life.

Lucy, the other children, and the great lion Aslan fret about being sent back from Narnia into the old world:

Lucy said, "We're so afraid of being sent away, Aslan. And you have sent us back into our own world so often."

"No fear of that," said Aslan. "Have you not guessed?"

Their hearts leaped and a wild hope rose within them.

"There *was* a real railway accident," said Aslan softly. "Your father and mother and all of you are—as you used to call it in the Shadow-Lands—dead. The term is over: the holidays have begun. The dream is ended: this is the morning." (*The Last Battle*, p. 183)

Pure faith does not need an image, or even an analogy. But for those of us well seasoned in doubt and in need of some picture or intellectual framework, we hurry to the imagination in search of some context in which to understand the mystery of resurrection. Death, at a natural level, has such finality. The corruption of the body, the absence of a familiar voice, and the loss of companionship all overwhelm our finite attempts to extract meaning from such darkness. What, if anything, lies beyond death's dark door?

When I receive notice that someone whom I have known has died, I often send to the family and friends of the deceased the following two poems by Jessica Powers. These verses brought comfort to my soul when my parents, one of my sisters, and my brother died. The imagery and theology speak deeply and accurately of the mystery of resurrection:

"The Homecoming"
The spirit, newly freed from earth,
is all amazed at the surprise
of her belonging: suddenly
as native to eternity
to see herself, to realize
the heritage that lets her be
at home where all this glory lies.

By naught foretold could she have guessed
such welcome home: the robe, the ring,
music and endless banqueting,
these people hers; this place of rest
known, as of long remembering
herself a child of God and pressed
with warm endearments to His breast.

"The Great Mystery"
My uncle had one sober comment for
all deaths. Well, he (or she)
has, he would say, solved the great mystery.
I tried as child to pierce the dark unknown,
straining to reach the keyhole of that door,
massive and grave, through which one slips alone.

A little girl is mostly prophecy.
And here, as there before,
when fact arrests me at that solemn door,
I reach and find the keyhole still too high,
though now I can surmise that it will be
light (and not darkness) that will meet the eye.
  (Regina Siegfried and Robert F. Morneau,
    eds., *Selected Poetry of Jessica Powers*,
      pp. 53, 100)

## "Felix Lives" (In memory of Br. Felix Scanlon)

Felix lives
in life beyond our conceiving.
While we pray here
the spirits are wiping not only tears
but fuzz from his eyes.
He was a man bemused and befuddled,
scarcely knowing the men
who loved and reached out to him,
but now it is revelation itself
that clears his eyes
and dismisses the shadows around him.
The glory is shining
on unrolling parchment
where he reads the new order of love,
where there is no more forgetting,
only new knowing
and hands outstretched to lead him
to the Lord of all living.

- What metaphors or images speak to you of resurrection?
  Write, paint, or draw them. Imagine your resurrection.
- Talk with Jesus or some other wisdom figure about how to
  live out of the Shadow-Lands and in the light now. How
  can you let the "Lord of all living" stretch out his arms to
  you now?

## "The Eyes of the Dead"

The dead have eyes and they watch
as I turn the poet's pages.
Out of the night overhanging
like a great oak tree
they peer in on me as I feel
a light wind rising.
I feel there is something strange
on the shelves where my books are resting,
something strange like love,
something unlike the ennui
that weighs like wet cloth upon me.

I know that the eyes of the dead
are resting upon me,
a tenderness like soft leaves
curling in at the window,
a grace that is drawing me close,
ever closer, to Beauty.

- Invite tender, grace-filled, resurrected loved ones to be with you.
- Rest in silence. Close your eyes. Imagine the garden, the new Eden, that Jesus reclaimed through the Resurrection. Stroll there with your loved ones. Let your heart sing with hope.

❧  ❧  ❧

# Calling

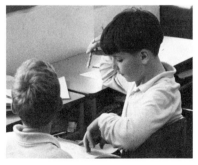

## ❧ 11 ❧

# The Call to Friendship

**Opening Prayer**

Holy Friend, teach me to be the type of loyal, wise, and generous friend that I hope for when I meet other women and men. Warm my soul with a passion for loving friendship.

# Hymn

Celebrate not birthdays
but your days of tallest living.
Save your candles not for the tenth or the twentieth year
of calendared onliving
but to memorialize those meetings at white tables
when low music played
as you looked long into your friend's eyes, knowing
the leap and thrust of friendship.
Celebrate the day of second coming
when your friend raised you to his height
and you, as one together, saw the meat and wine
and ferns and flowers in a new light swimming.
Celebrate not passage of the years
but those few crests of time
when love and friendship came
and touched and gently lifted.

("Celebrations")

# God's Word

Naomi then said, "Look, your sister-in-law has gone back to her people and to her god. Go home, too; follow your sister-in-law."

But Ruth said, "Do not press me to leave you and to stop going with you, for

wherever you go, I shall go,
wherever you live, I shall live.
Your people will be my people,
and your God will be my God.
Where you die, I shall die
and there I shall be buried.
Let Yahweh bring unnameable ills on me
and worse ills, too,
if anything but death
should part me from you!"

Seeing that Ruth was determined to go with her, Naomi said no more. (Ruth 1:15–18)

**Pause**: Ponder and be grateful for the friends who go where you go, who refuse to be parted from you.

# Reading

Is that [diffidence at one's power and promise] the basis of friendship? Is it as reactive as that? Was our friendship for the Langs born out of simple gratitude to this woman who had the kindness to call on a strange young wife stuck in a basement without occupation or friends? Was I that avid for praise, to feel so warm toward them both because they professed to like my story? Do we all buzz or ring or light up when people press our vanity buttons, and only then? Can I think of anyone in my whole life whom I have liked without his [her] first showing signs of liking me? Or did I (I hope I did) like Charity Lang on sight because she was what she was, open, friendly, frank, a little ribald as it turned out, energetic, interested, as full of vitality as her smile was full of light? (Wallace Stegner, *Crossing to Safety,* p. 18)

# Canticle

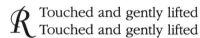

℟ Touched and gently lifted
Touched and gently lifted

Friendship, crests of time peaking over all others
Days heightened, living forever, giving vision
Crescendos that hold aloft the meaning of life

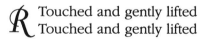

℟ Touched and gently lifted
Touched and gently lifted

Friendship, ferns and flowers nourishing the hunger for beauty
Meat and wine inebriating the spirit
Words and glances bonding the distance

℟ Touched and gently lifted
Touched and gently lifted

Friendship, birthdays too far apart—celebrate now
Anniversaries, too often forgotten—celebrate now
Death, too soon approaching—celebrate now

℟ Touched and gently lifted
  Touched and gently lifted

**Closing Prayer**

God of all good gifts,
what treasures have been poured out of your glass of blessings:
music and memories and new-mown hay.
Yet what can compare with friendship, the gift of sheer grace?
Teach us to celebrate the mystery of love and affinity.
Gently lift us to the heights of union
with you and with those we love.
Give us days of tall living.
Amen. Alleluia!

# *Food for Meditation, Journaling, or Sharing*

## *Reflection*

At some point in my study of philosophy, I stumbled across a
word in Josef Pieper's *Leisure, the Basis of Culture:* "connatu-
rality." The word refers to the human experience of oneness,
congruence, affinity. Some people know death or God through
study and reflection. Others experience these mysteries deep
in the heart—connaturally. This word seemed to me to apply
to friendship, the experience when two people discover that
they see the same thing, feel deeply the same events of life,
and have the ability to share the vision and excitement together.

Friendship has more intensity than temporality. Good
friends do not need long times together. Rather, when they do
meet, their intense affection deepens and lasts, suffering the
vicissitudes of fragile existence with ease. Intense friendship
creates a safe zone for the bonding of hearts. Timing when to

come and when to go indicates an authentic and healthy friendship.

Friendship is a grace freely given, nonenforceable. It comes like a shooting star lighting up the dark unexpectedly. It transforms like the first day of spring chasing winter back to the north. Friendship is the pleasure of presence in storm and sun that allows us to thrive.

## "A Man Ignited"

When friendship struck he was a man ignited.
It seemed there was new flame within him
bidding him rise and speak
as he had not risen and spoken
through all the slack and sullen days.
He wrote and his lines told a tale
of friendship like new fire
crackling within him that would not let him rest,
so that it was not strange for him
to sit at table with two friends
all through the night until the fringe of dawn.
It was not strange for him to speak
as he had never spoken
to brother, sister, teacher, parent.

He talked and drank, invoking poets, artists,
all masters of the spirit,
of how he cherished Yeats
and loved *The Four Quartets*.
There was no limit to his ranging vision.
He spoke and saw his friends' eyes widen
all through the riches of that strangest night
which closed at dawn with his two friends saying
"this was indeed a man ignited."

- Recall a time when being with a friend "ignited" your soul and heart, and time seemed to stand still. Sing praise for this experience.
- Reflect on a friendless time. How did you feel? Pray about it.

## "Beginning of Friendship"

Beginning is always the best,
the instant knowing,
the twist of the dial to gladness,
the stepping out to a clearing flanked by trees
eerily new but familiar.
You have been there before. You remember the light
as you remember the smile that steals into you.
You take the hands remembering the hands
stretched out to you in old mornings.
This is best, you say, as out of memory
you step with him into the daylight.

- Remember and meditate on the beginnings of significant friendships. Give thanks for the gladness.
- Consider new friends and people who you would like to begin a friendship with. Talk with God about your hope.

## ❧ 12 ❧

# The Call to Eucharist

### Opening Prayer

Living God, you sent your son Jesus to be our nourishment, our sustenance for the journey. Now may we be bread for the journey of our sisters and brothers.

# Hymn

In Easter Week divinity waits
half hidden in the bushes, its
pale gold behind the buds, a magic
to be missed by half-shut eyes.
On the white beach the red coals burn
with fish and bread upon them
and strong hands that have passed through wind and stone.
At this table where spring flowers are glassed,
bread and meat and fruit wait
for the gathering of the brothers,
and they will sit where divinity is waiting,
and some of them will know it
in the breaking of the bread.

("Fragment for Easter Week")

# God's Word

While [Jesus] was with them at table, he took the bread and said the blessing; then he broke it and handed it to them. And their eyes were opened and they recognised him; but he had vanished from their sight. Then they said to each other, "Did not our hearts burn within us as he talked to us on the road and explained the scriptures to us?"

They set out that instant and returned to Jerusalem. There they found the Eleven assembled together with their companions, who said to them, "[Christ] has indeed risen and has appeared to Simon." Then they told their story of what had happened on the road and how they had recognised him at the breaking of bread. (Luke 24:30–35)

**Pause**: Have you encountered Christ in the breaking of bread with your sisters and brothers?

# Reading

The Eucharistic life is not a devotional addition to existence but the clue to all real existence whether social or personal. It is concerned with the mighty realities of evil and redemption, death and life. (Evelyn Underhill, *An Anthology of the Love of God,* p. 162)

"Consecration"
Upon the paten, Lord, each morn I place
    This heart of mine.
Say over it the changing word Thou sayest
    Over bread and wine.
'Twill purge it of its waywardness and make
    It wholly thine.
    (Ruth Mary Fox, *Some Did Return,* p. 131)

# Canticle

  ℟ In the breaking of the bread
    In the breaking of the bread

Divinity waits to shout "surprise"
Divinity longs for intimate conversation
Divinity delights in banishing uncertainty
Divinity sustains the lonely and forgotten
Divinity commissions bakers to feed the world

  ℟ In the breaking of the bread
    In the breaking of the bread

The despondent recover hope
The lost find a home
The confused see a guiding light
The weary meet enthusiasm
The fearful are gifted with strength

  ℟ In the breaking of the bread
    In the breaking of the bread

**Closing Prayer**

God of bread and life,
you long to feed the people formed by your hand.
Draw us to your seashore
and speak deeply to our heart.
Grant us the grace to recognize you
wherever bread is broken,
wherever love is offered,
wherever compassion is shared.
Then our praise will be sincere,
and our thanksgiving holy.
We pray this in Jesus, the bread of life.
Amen. Alleluia.

# *Food for Meditation, Journaling, or Sharing*

## *Reflection*

Ultimately, we confront the God question, the question of
divinity vis-à-vis humanity. Atheists try to exempt themselves
from the question by denying the subject. But for those of us
startled by infinity and by a sense of a creator behind creation,
the hunt is on. It ends only when some answer is secured or
death intervenes.

Even so, we may be studying the stars from the wrong
end of the telescope. Maybe God quests for humanity, and the
suspense of the story comes from seeing if the creature has
the wisdom, courage, and humility to stop running long
enough to be embraced by the Source of its being.

This is no hide-and-go-seek farce, but a matter of recognition and response. Can divinity be experienced in the breaking of the bread, in the healing of a wounded heart, in the
forgiving of deep hurt, in the sheltering of the homeless, in
the counseling of the confused? Could divinity be too incarnate, so that we have lost the ability to see the obvious?

At home or church, the table speaks of life, companionship, food, conversation, communion, and joy. When eucharistic, the table becomes the intersection of divinity and

humanity. Bread broken and shared, life claimed and given, love received and distributed give us an assurance that God continues to dwell with us. Praise and thanksgiving are the only appropriate responses.

## "Sacrament"

He looked upon the drab mouths,
the level eyes of the slow-moving.
These men had taken life itself in their hands
and raised it to unfeeling lips.
He wondered that this could be,
this ritual of the uncaring,
this solemnity of the sober,
the impotent before the Electric,
the dancing sun we call God.

Strangely he saw himself dancing
(in delicate vision he saw it),
dancing with others, men and women
disporting themselves like children.
The Son of God led the dance
under archways laden with gold.
They rejoiced in the bread they had eaten,
this life that sang within them.
They danced and never grew weary
of the new life springing within them.

- Should we not dance and sing to celebrate the Eucharist? Rejoice in some way for the bread of life.
- Sing "Lord of the Dance" or "How Can I Keep from Singing?" If you are moved to, sway and dance before your God.

## "Holy Thursday 1967"

Having loved his own who were in the world
he loves them to the end
so that he kneels, his rough cloak thrown aside,
in Harlem or in Congo or in Vietnam tonight,
bathing his brothers' feet,
bending to bind them.

While Excellencies and Eminences
dine daintily and alone
he on his hands and knees
pours water on the bruised
and scorched and mangled feet
of those so numbed and dazed with pain
they cannot see the soothing hands.

They cannot rest, the unremitting
hands, laid on the feet
that marched for justice, held
on flesh burnt raw by napalm fire.
They cannot rest till they who call
him master kneel with him
and stoop with joy to bathe and bind
their brothers' sacred feet.

- Conduct an examen of consciousness with this question:
  Whose sacred feet do I need to wash?
- Seek God's grace for the power to bind your companions'
  feet.

~ *13* ~

# The Call to Worship

## Opening Prayer

Wonderful God, only our pride keeps us from breaking out in song at your glory. May we come before you in awe like the Magi, like children, like wise elders and give you worship. All praise to you, God with us.

# Hymn

Pentecost! What has it meant to you and to me?
Frankly, I haven't seen any tongues of fire lately
or doves on my window-sill cooing and urging me
to tall love and to inspired living.
What does Pentecost mean to little old ladies
at church doors passing out pamphlets
or moldy old men at the street corners
lost in their thoughts?
No, the Spirit has not unfolded himself and his rapture
to you or to me in this downtrodden city.

But it has, not in flames or in feathers,
but in opulent silence when alone near the window.
I prayed with all the power that was in me,
and into the silence stepped the three that I loved,
a man and two women, come out of death to touch me.
The Spirit was like splendid silver
as he held me there fast in my love.

Yes, it has come as I happily remember
the group that I loved.
I sat with them praying and listening,
not marking the time.
Suddenly joy rippled over us, touching our lips
and bidding us rise to embrace
the arms and transcendent shoulders.
We were quite unprepared for glory,
a people clothed with the Spirit.

("Pentecost")

# God's Word

When Pentecost day came round, they had all met together,
when suddenly there came from heaven a sound as of a
violent wind which filled the entire house in which they were
sitting; and there appeared to them tongues as of fire; these
separated and came to rest on the head of each of them. They

were all filled with the Holy Spirit and began to speak different languages as the Spirit gave them power to express themselves. (Acts 2:1–4)

**Pause:** Recall a time when the Spirit filled you. How did you express yourself and the Spirit within you?

# Reading

Not only prayer . . . gives God glory but work. Smiting on an anvil, sawing a beam, . . . sweeping, scouring, everything gives God some glory if being in his grace you do it as your duty. To go to communion worthily gives God great glory, but to take food in thankfulness and temperance gives him glory too. To lift up the hands in prayer gives God glory, but a man with a dungfork in his hand, a woman with a sloppail, give him glory too. He is so great that all things give him glory if you mean they should. (Rainer Maria Rilke, *Poems from the Book of Hours*, p. 4)

# Canticle

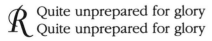 Quite unprepared for glory
Quite unprepared for glory

Peter, the chosen who turned denier
John, the beloved who saw an empty tomb
Nathaniel, the guileless wounded by the cross
James, the son of thunder angered by life
Mary, the mother pierced by the sword of sorrow

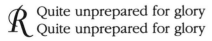 Quite unprepared for glory
Quite unprepared for glory

Francis of Assisi, in brown poverty and battle scars
Teresa of Ávila, writing in silence and solitude
Catherine of Siena, politically active and prayerful
Teresa of Calcutta, streetwise and contemplative
Augustine of Hippo, confessing God's glory and human sin

℞ Quite unprepared for glory
℞ Quite unprepared for glory

Alan Paton, who cried the beloved country
Thomas Merton, who climbed the seven-storey mountain
Dorothy Day, a Catholic worker and lover
Martin Luther King, Jr., seer of dreams and advocate of justice
Dietrich Bonhoeffer, a disciple who paid the cost

℞ Quite unprepared for glory
℞ Quite unprepared for glory

**Closing Prayer**

God of glory,
we find you not in flames and feather
but in the lives of your people.
Your revelation shines forth in the deeds of all who hear your
     voice.
Teach us silence and how to stand alone near quiet windows.
Instruct us in your way of truth, love, justice, and freedom.
Then, glorified by your love,
our lives will become radiant and transparent.
Then light, your glory, will again dawn in our darkness.
Amen. Alleluia!

# *Food for Meditation, Journaling, or Sharing*

## *Reflection*

Our calendars once highlighted religious feasts: Advent waiting, Christmas joy, Epiphany light, Lenten fasts, Easter alleluias. Now it seems that calendars tout strictly secular doings: Memorial Day, Fourth of July, Labor Day, and all the ubiquitous seasons of sports—baseball, football, hockey, basketball, and golf. Television guides our rhythm of life. Too easily we become the creatures of commercials. We excuse ourselves for a leisurely rest or a long, sound sleep. Our "culture" shapes our destiny.

Some groups hold out against the onslaught of mainstream culture. Hewing close to treasured customs and tended land, the Amish confuse us as they drive by silently in their black buggies. But most religious groups have witnessed the erosion of the meanings of their images and symbols.

A defensive posture does not serve as the best strategy. The challenge is to discern and appropriate the light wherever it shines, even if dimly, and to draw others together with us in the search. To retain our humanity, we must seek our God where the sacred can be found, whatever the season or shape of grace. Then, when we ritualize these glory moments, we make the light shine brighter.

## *"Holy Saturday"*

This is the day most aptly ours,
the solemnizing of the time
of brooding, the never to be ended
liturgy of waiting,
this day of the entombed means most
to us the always hoping. The Holy One
we have not seen speaks gently
to us from the stone.
We think of him who lies, like us,
enclosed. We look to one another
for the sudden cut of breakthrough
and the swift incision in the stone.

- Recall times when sacred days like Holy Saturday have urged you to worship, to seek God in new ways, and to ponder people in a fresh way.
- Reflect on your sources of hope. Pray for hope in areas where you need it most. Give praise and thanks for hope where you find it.

## *"Sunday"*

Sunday (O Lord) is rest
and newspapers stacked or strewn,
wine on the table and taste
of veal through the afternoon.

Sunday (O Lord) is strolling
through sunbaked parks, the play
of whining children (their yawning
fathers smile at the close of this day).

Sunday is listening to Brahms
half asleep in a well draped room,
the rustling of pages like rustle
of mice in a tomb.

Sunday (O Lord) is for rest,
bowed head, and the easy chair;
the day of peace when your children
fret and your absence is everywhere.

- Examine how you spend your Sundays. How can your
  leisure be worship? Or does Sunday become a day to work?
- Spend a Sunday looking at the small miracles in your life.
  As soon as you see one, say, "Thank you, God!"

## ❦ 14 ❦

# The Call to Teach

### Opening Prayer

Holy Wisdom, may I always dine at your table. Open my mind and heart to your wisdom wherever I encounter it—with teachers and friends, in books or nature. Teach me your ways.

# Hymn

It begins in the sparkle of firstness—
the well swept aisles, clean slate, and unlined paper,
open doors and windows,
and thirty silent watchers.
It all begins in fumbling,
the miscues, the missteps of the first days,
and there is the vastness, the breathless heat of September,
and there are the eyes of the watchers.

Now in the font of September is freshness.
We half believe
that it will stay with us the cleanness,
the brittle silence.
We half believe that the watchers
will never move out of that glassed
illusion, the first days.

("The First Days")

# God's Word

Jesus, with the power of the Spirit in him, returned to Galilee;
and his reputation spread throughout the countryside. He
taught in their synagogues and everyone glorified him.

He came to Nazara, where he had been brought up, and
went into the synagogue on the Sabbath day as he usually did.
He stood up to read, and they handed him the scroll of the
prophet Isaiah. Unrolling the scroll he found the place where
it is written:

The spirit of the Lord is on me,
for he has anointed me
to bring the good news to the afflicted.
He has sent me to proclaim liberty to captives,
sight to the blind,
to let the oppressed go free,
to proclaim a year of favour from the Lord.

(Luke 4:14–19)

**Pause**: In your own way, who do you teach about the
Good News?

# Reading

Near the close of his address, Mark Van Doren told this group that when he took hold of the doorknob of his own classroom to enter it for his lectures, he always paused. It was holy ground, a holy opportunity! Would he be able to measure up to it? Can we be given the grace to help to share in his anticipatory awe? (Douglas V. Steere, *Together in Solitude,* p. 40)

# Canticle

R In the sparkle of firstness
In the sparkle of firstness

The garden, now seeded with no weed in sight
The car, with the smell of factory newness
The glance, love at first sight with its idealism
The office, first day at the desk and all in neat order
The puppy, a ball of enthusiasm and absolute trust

R In the sparkle of firstness
In the sparkle of firstness

The snowfall, in its pristine loveliness
The dwelling, newly built, awaiting occupancy
The conscience, innocent of cruelty or selfishness
The newborn, announcing its arrival into the human community

R In the sparkle of firstness
In the sparkle of firstness

**Closing Prayer**

God of newness,
source of pristine beauty,
our first experiences of life bode well the future.
Too soon our selfishness discolors life,
our deeds often filled with exploitation and manipulation.
The earth is now scarred,
the water, the pure water, contaminated,
the air filled with foul elements,

the fire burning now with too much hate.
Send us teachers
who share the firstness of life,
the purity of freshness,
that your glory may be manifest
and our praise sincere.
Amen. Alleluia!

# Food for Meditation, Journaling, or Sharing

## Reflection

A bottle of carbonated soda loses its fizz and tang when exposed to the open air. The sparkle of teaching can dissipate as the semesters move on, too. But another first day hides just around the corner, and the adventure of learning begins afresh. The Creation story is repeated any time that someone teaches.

Our school sat on a hill. That first day of first grade in 1944, with Sister Jean Marie as my teacher, held minor fears and diminutive apprehensions, but also excitement and adventure. School offered me a new world of words and numbers, maps and facts, mysteries and dreams.

Ever since that first day, whether as a student or a teacher, each term begins with a sparkle of firstness and freshness for me. As the pencils dulled, the erasers filled with chalk dust, the classes grew routine, the freshness wore off. Nevertheless, the first day always offered an aroma of marvelous possibilities.

Teaching, that process of information, formation, and transformation, has never been clearly defined to my satisfaction. It is a lot like love, too mysterious and complex to yield to the world of explanation. Even so, we know what it is and when it is done well or poorly. At the end of a class or course, if we sense order, see connections, and desire to return again, the miracle of learning has taken place.

Everyone should compose a list of teachers who have offered them wisdom and encouragement for life's journey. A fifth grade teacher who talked of Newton and his fall from gravity; a biology teacher who praised the amoeba and then helped us discover it under a microscope; a professor whose demand that Hopkins be memorized and recited led to a change of inner landscape; a graduate school mentor who required excellence and demonstrated the joys of thorough research. Praise be all teachers, great and small, and the sparkle of newness and firstness that they share.

## "The Teacher"

The eyes,
the two and thirty pairs of them
he would not see close up again,
and yet for all they yielded
of the crackling fire within
they might as well have been that many stars
peering across the space-years.

He remembered now the laughter
of their teeth, the simulated
pleasure in his wit,
and all the while they looked
across cool distances
at this grotesque who leaned and smiled
to them against the years.

And still he hoped as the new eyes came
and peered across the time-gorge at him,
that some day they would meet,
they and he enclosed in this one room.

- Recall the teachers whose mind and heart met yours. Thank God for them.
- Who do you teach? What do you teach?

## "The Last Days"

And what is Oedipus to them,
the choral cry, the diviners,
the oracles of self-slaying?
What are these to the young men
straining now in the last days?
What are these to the young men
now that the windows open
on fresh gales, the waiting motors,
the wheels of spring?

What can we say to them now
in these last few modules of order
as they sit here tensed to take off,
fling themselves behind wheels,
and bolt into life without limit
or measure or time or precision?

There is nothing to say to them now.
The ancient wisdom must wait,
the seers, the chorus of elders,
and the Fates that crouch in the shadows.

- Action and learning often seem at odds. Do you ever feel
  this tension? How do you maintain balance?
- What ancient wisdom influences your life? How do teachers
  such as the Bible, good novels, and serious movies help
  you grow to full living?

## ❧ 15 ❧

# The Call to Live

## Opening Prayer

Creator of the universe, you created us for full, glorious living.
Seduce me from destruction; propel me to awe. As the sun
surely rises each morning, I praise your hope for humanity
and pledge my soul to love and living.

# Hymn

In this house I am the one man
stirring. Even the sun has not made it
over the chimneys. God sits still
at his place taking my measure.
Now as I crouch here, dull before coffee,
before the drawing of drapes, of dreams
from my eyes, now before Genesis,
now as the sleepers lie before being
created again and breathed upon
to new living.
Let me say to him who has roused me:
"I sit here half-dazed in this room in the house
of the world. I do not know why you roused me
out of forebeing. You sit there
a cat on the sill ever watching.
Day after day I rise to you asking:
Who am I, Lord? What are you?
And when will it come, my rising
and you and I speaking?"

("At Rising")

# God's Word

"Look, today I [Moses] am offering you life and prosperity,
death and disaster. If you obey the commandments of Yahweh
your God, . . . if you love Yahweh your God, . . . if you
keep [the] commandments . . . you will live and grow nu-
merous, and Yahweh your God will bless you. . . . I am
offering you life or death, blessing or curse. Choose life, then,
so that you and your descendants may live, in the love of
Yahweh your God." (Deut. 30:15–20)

**Pause:** Bring to mind as many blessings as you can that
grace your day; then say yes to them.

# Reading

The web of our life is of a mingled yarn, good and ill together; our virtues would be proud if our faults whipp'd them not,
and our crimes would despair if they were not cherish'd by
our virtues. (William Shakespeare, *All's Well That Ends Well,*
act 4, sc. 3, ll. 68–71)

# Canticle

R Before the drawing of the drapes in morning
Before the drawing of the drapes in morning

The world sits in darkness, brooding
Dreams are free to play, unimpeded
The streets are silent, expectant
The sparrow hides in the pine, lonely
The houses are quiet, waiting

R Before the drawing of the drapes in morning
Before the drawing of the drapes in morning

Comes the question of who-ness: the enigma of self
Comes the question of why-ness: the mystery of being
Comes the question of time-ness: the paradox of
    successiveness
Comes the question of space-ness: the principle of place
Comes the question of what-ness: the employment of energies

R Before the drawing of the drapes in morning
Before the drawing of the drapes in morning

**Closing Prayer**

Why have you awakened me, good God,
into being, into this day, into this place?
Are you always so silent, before and after dawn,
or is it that I fail to hear?
Draw me into fullness and being,
speaking your love and demands before sunrise,
take your measure, but only with love's cup.

Then I will cry out with the psalmist:
"and with the dawn rejoicing!"
Amen. Alleluia!

# Food for Meditation, Journaling, or Sharing

## Reflection

In Willa Cather's *Death Comes for the Archbishop,* old Father Latour says about his eminent death: "I shall not die of a cold, my son. I shall die of having lived" (p. 269). Death draws the drapes and ends temporal light and activity. The cords that do the closing may be illness, but for the blessed, dying results from living life to the full, with nothing more to do or be.

An eighty-five-year-old woman whom I had known for six years fell and broke her wrist. The day after hearing of her fall, I received the news of her death. In mourning her loss, I concluded that the broken bone had not caused her death. I believe that her heart was so full of love for her friends and family that it just could not grow any more. The fruit was ripe; the harvester came.

At another point in Cather's novel, two aged French missionaries are reflecting on their decades of ministry in New Mexico:

"But it has not been so bad, Jean? We have done the things we used to plan to do, long ago, when we were Seminarians,—at least some of them. To fulfil the dreams of one's youth; that is the best that can happen to a man. No worldly success can take the place of that." (P. 261)

Indeed, after fulfilling the dreams, the drapes can be drawn in peace.

The real danger is a half-life filled with half-commitments, half-efforts, half-desires.

## "Personality Questionnaire"

Through afternoon and still another
morning the inquisitors
anonymous dwarfs, are asking:
Do you like to lie alone?
Are you ever ashamed of your dreams?

Now with a pin I prick my choice
irrelevancy, now with a pencil
I black out the one
from multiple evasions of the truth.

Through afternoon and yet another
morning they will never ask
what vision moves me at half-waking,
what I see when Mahler plays,
my one prayer when wrapped in pain.

The young inquisitors keep tapping
with their little questions. Let
them tap. I shall not open. I
stand guard half-smiling at this door.

- What is your dream, the vision that moves you and gives
  you energy? Share it with someone to whom it would mean
  a lot.
- What is your one prayer when wrapped in pain?

## "The Treasure"

The old man in late winter
is ruffled by winds out of oak trees.
His scuffed shoes shuffle the pavement
that winds around the new houses,
saplings, and covered gardens.
The old man would cry, if he dared,
of the spring that has fallen upon him,
of the treasure he hides within him.

"Many waters cannot quench,
neither can the floods drown it,"
he sings softly as Solomon sang.
"My treasure has come in the bleak years,
the lone years. It has come
in the days after hoping
to enrich beyond a youth's hoping."

The old man presses close to him
the gift that is stronger than death,
the jewel that burns within him,
burns away the years and the sorrow,
a treasure that renders him kingly
walking through late winter sundown.

- What is the treasure that hides deep within you, your source of hope? Bring it out and name it.
- Pray to always be able to see the spring in life, no matter what the season.

**Acknowledgments** *(continued)*

The quote on page 15 is from *Towards the Mountain: An Autobiography,* by Alan Paton (New York: Charles Scribner's Sons, 1980), page 59. Copyright © 1980 by Alan Paton. Used with permission of Scribner's, an imprint of Simon and Schuster.

The quote on pages 20–21 is from *The Sacred Journey,* by Frederick Buechner (San Francisco: Harper and Row, 1982), page 52. Copyright © 1982 by Frederick Buechner.

Br. Edward Seifert's poem "Integrity," on pages 23–24, first appeared in *English Journal,* vol. 56, November 1967, page 1152. Copyright © 1967 by the National Council of Teachers of English.

The quote by Saint Thomas Aquinas on page 27 is from *Saint-Watching,* by Phyllis McGinley (New York: Viking Press, 1961), page 7. Copyright © 1969 by Phyllis McGinley.

The quote by Goethe on page 27 is from *Faust,* edited by Walter Kaufmann (Garden City, NY: Doubleday and Co., 1961), page 217. Copyright © 1961 by Walter Kaufmann.

The excerpts by Wordsworth, Donne, Dunbar, Herbert, Rossetti, Shakespeare, Blake, Sidney, and Whitman on pages 27–28 are all taken from *The Columbia Granger's Dictionary of Poetry Quotations,* edited by Edith P. Hazen (New York: Columbia University Press, 1992), pages 509, 143, 152, 211, 379, 407, 53, 421, and 491, respectively. Copyright © 1992 by Columbia University Press.

The excerpt by Jessica Powers on page 27 is from *Mantras from a Poet: Jessica Powers,* by Robert F. Morneau (Kansas City, MO: Sheed and Ward, 1991), page 37. Copyright © 1991 by Robert F. Morneau. All rights reserved.

The excerpt on page 33 is from *Late Night Thoughts on Listening to Mahler's Ninth Symphony,* by Lewis Thomas (New York: Viking Press, 1980), page 105. Copyright © 1983 by Lewis Thomas.

Br. Edward Seifert's poems "Mozart in Motion," on pages 34–35, and "At Rising," on page 104, were originally published in *Sisters Today.*

The quote by Felix Marti-Ibañez on page 36 is from *The Crystal Arrow* (New York: Clarkson N. Potter, 1964), page xv. Copyright © 1964 by Felix Marti-Ibañez, MD.

The quote by May Sarton on page 38 is from *Journal of a Solitude* (New York: W. W. Norton, 1973), page 97. Copyright © 1973 by May Sarton.

The quote by George Eliot on page 38 is from *Adam Bede* (New York: New American Library, 1961), page 475. Copyright © 1961 by the New American Library of World Literature.

Br. Edward Seifert's poems "After My Silent Summer," on pages 39–40, and "Beginning of Friendship," on page 84, first appeared in *Crosscurrents,* Summer 1984.

The excerpt on page 47 is from *Anne Frank: The Diary of a Young Girl,* translated by B. M. Mooyaart-Doubleday (New York: Random House, 1952), page 172. Copyright © 1952 by Otto H. Frank.